Letterland

Interactive Handwriting Practice

This book belongs to:

....

Download the FREE app
Search 'Interactive Handwriting' on the App Store or scan this QR code. Available for iOS and Android.

Download on the App Store | GET IT ON Google Play

How to use this book

There are 52 basic letter shapes in written English (**Aa**–**Zz**) and they are all abstract shapes.

In Letterland these abstract shapes are linked to child-friendly characters that children love and quickly get to know. When your child sees the Letterland characters linked to the letter shapes, the risk of confusing all these abstract shapes is greatly reduced. You'll then find that even when you show the plain black letter shape your child will 'see' the character in their mind's eye, helping them remember the sound and how to form the letter shape.

It's important for your child to learn the right 'movement pathway' for each letter. Correct formation ensures that the letters begin and end in the right place. This is especially important when your child moves on to the next stages of joined-up handwriting. If young children are allowed to form letters 'their own way' these habits quickly become established and can be very difficult to correct later.

Finger-trace!
When little fingers get the habit of forminag each letter the right way handwriting becomes much easier. Let your child use their finger to trace over each large hollow letter before using the pencil to write the strokes. There are starting arrows to show the correct starting points.

Write and sing!
Search 'Interactive Handwriting' on the App Store to see the animated *Handwriting Songs*. Watch the letter shapes being formed on screen. The catchy tunes are full of easy-to-remember tips on creating the letter shapes. Trace over the large letter shapes first and then move onto smaller letters as skills improve.

Song lyrics
Each song provides a friendly rhyme to guide correct letter formation (both lower and uppercase). Sing along with the app as the letter shapes are formed.

Sentences and phrases
These short phrases allow your child to see the the target letter starting words. The pictures give them clues to remember the phrases. Read the words with your child emphasizing the target sound.

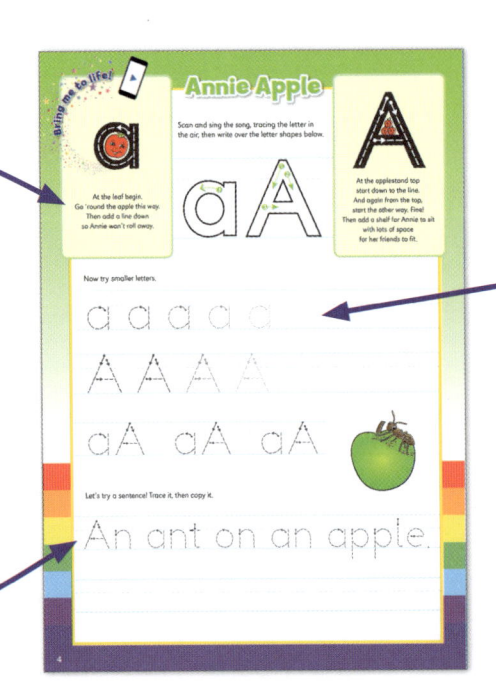

Handwriting practice
Dots and arrows to help with starting positions and correct letter formation. Letter shapes become more faint so children gradually learn to form letters on their own.

Warm up!

Let's warm up by tracing the lines below.

Annie Apple

Bring me to life!

At the leaf begin.
Go 'round the apple this way.
Then add a line down
so Annie won't roll away.

Scan and sing the song, tracing the letter in the air, then write over the letter shapes below.

At the applestand top
start down to the line.
And again from the top,
start the other way. Fine!
Then add a shelf for Annie to sit
with lots of space
for her friends to fit.

Now try smaller letters.

a a a a a

A A A A A

aA aA aA aA

Let's try a sentence! Trace it, then copy it.

An ant on an apple.

Bouncy Ben

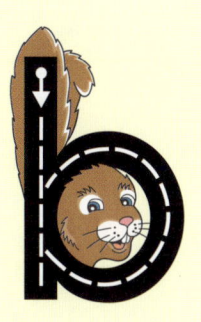

Brush down Ben's big, long ears. Go up and 'round his head so his face appears.

Scan and sing the song, tracing the letter in the air, then write over the letter shapes below.

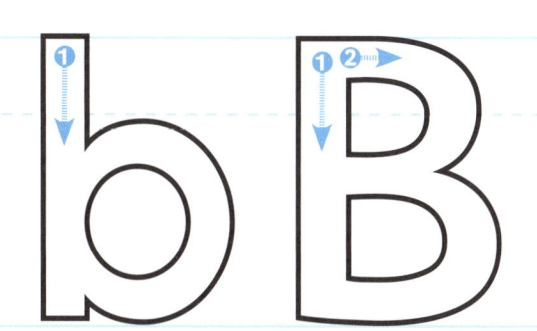

b B

Brush down Bouncy Ben's big brown ear, Then go 'round his balancing ball, Next brush gently 'round his head, but take care that his ball won't fall.

Now try smaller letters.

b b b b b

B B B B B

bB   bB   bB

Let's try a sentence! Trace it, then copy it.

A bag by a bell.

Clever Cat

Bring me to life!

Curve 'round Clever Cat's face to begin. Then gently tickle her under her chin.

Scan and sing the song, tracing the letter in the air, then write over the letter shapes below.

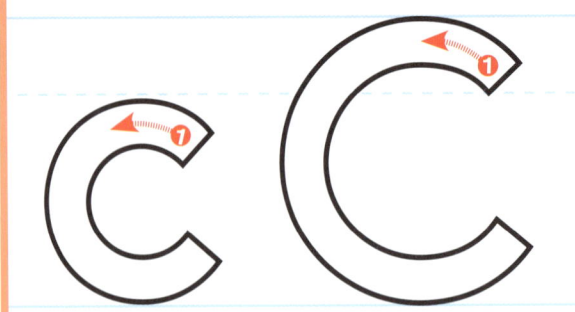

Come, make a BIG curve 'round Clever Cat's face, to show us her letter when it's uppercase.

Now try smaller letters.

Let's try a sentence! Trace it, then copy it.

A cat and a cup.

Dippy Duck

Draw Dippy Duck's back.
Go 'round her tum.
Go up to her head.
Then down you come!

Scan and sing the song, tracing the letter in the air, then write over the letter shapes below.

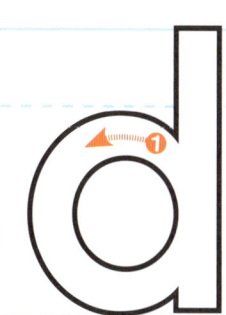

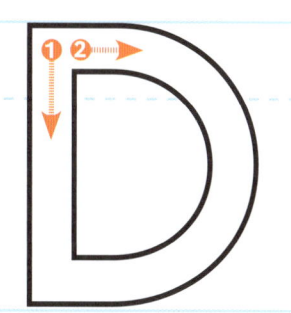

Draw down from the top of
Dippy Duck's door.
Go all the way down to the floor.
Then start at the top once more.
Curve down to the ground
for a funny-shaped door.

Now try smaller letters.

Let's try a sentence! Trace it, then copy it.

A dog and a drum.

Bring me to life!

Eddy Elephant

Scan and sing the song, tracing the letter in the air, then write over the letter shapes below.

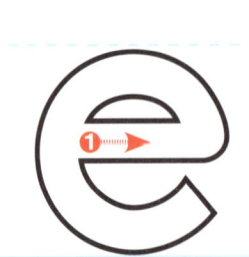

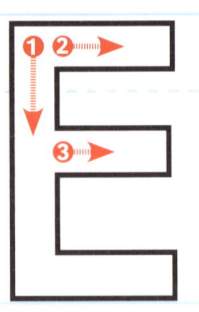

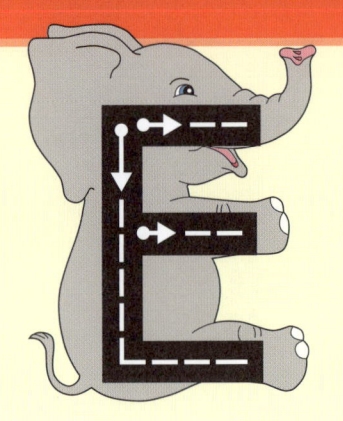

Ed has a headband. Draw it and then stroke 'round his head and his trunk to the end.

Eddy Elephant loves sitting on end. Draw down from his head to his leg at the end. Draw a line for his trunk, and one leg in the air. That's how to make Eddy sitting right there!

Now try smaller letters.

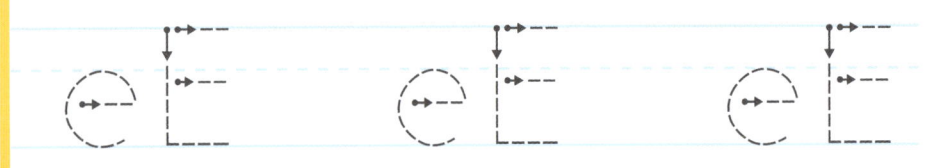

e e e e e

E E E E E

eE eE eE

Let's try a sentence! Trace it, then copy it.

Eggs in egg cups.

8

Firefighter Fred

Scan and sing the song, tracing the letter in the air, then write over the letter shapes below.

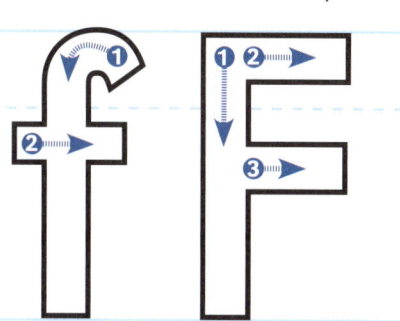

First draw Fred's helmet. Then go down a way. Give him some arms and he'll put out the blaze.

For uppercase Firefighter Fred, go down to his feet from his head. Go across at his helmet. Then add his arm, so he'll use his hose to keep us from harm.

Now try smaller letters.

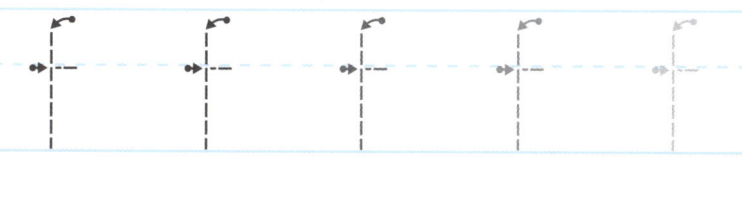

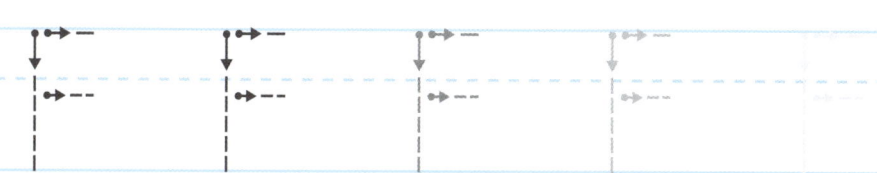

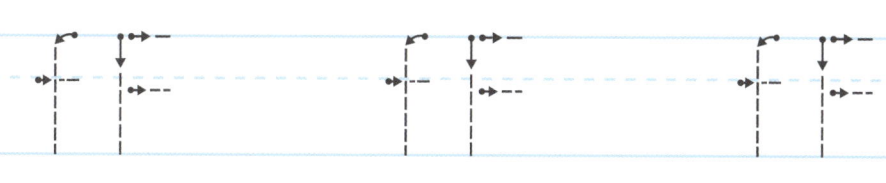

f   f   f   f   f

F   F   F   F   F

fF   fF   fF   fF

Let's try a sentence! Trace it, then copy it.

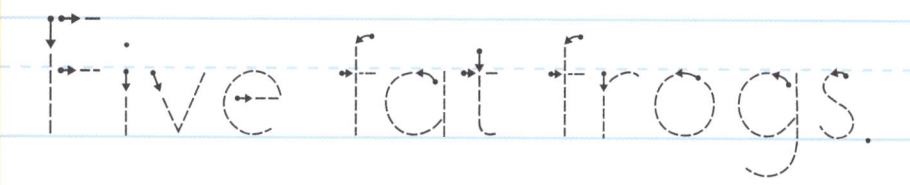

Five fat frogs.

Golden Girl

Bring me to life!

Go 'round Golden Girl's head.
Go down her golden hair.
Then curve to make her swing,
so she can sit there.

Scan and sing the song, tracing the letter in the air, then write over the letter shapes below.

gG

Go 'round in nearly a circle to draw Golden Girl's fast go-cart. Go across with a short straight line, so her go-cart is ready to start.

Now try smaller letters.

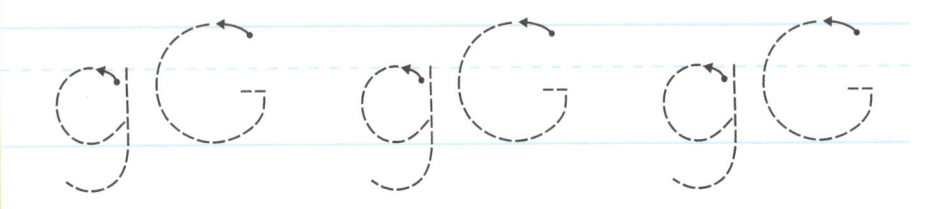

g g g g g

G G G G

gG gG gG

Let's try a sentence! Trace it, then copy it.

A goat by a gate.

Harry Hat Man

Hurry from the Hat Man's head down to his heel on the ground. Go up and bend his knee over so he'll hop while he makes his sound.

Scan and sing the song, tracing the letter in the air, then write over the letter shapes below.

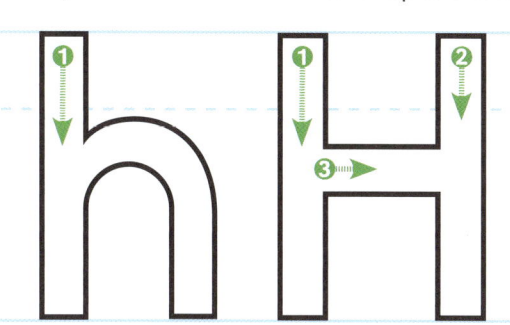

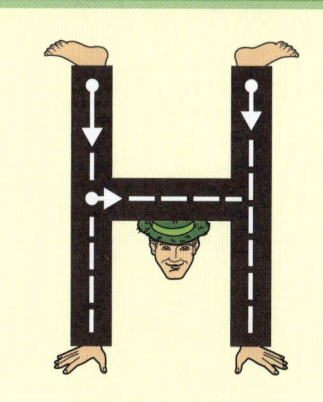

Hurry from heel to hand, then again from heel to hand. Then add a line across for the Hat Man's big handstand!

Now try smaller letters.

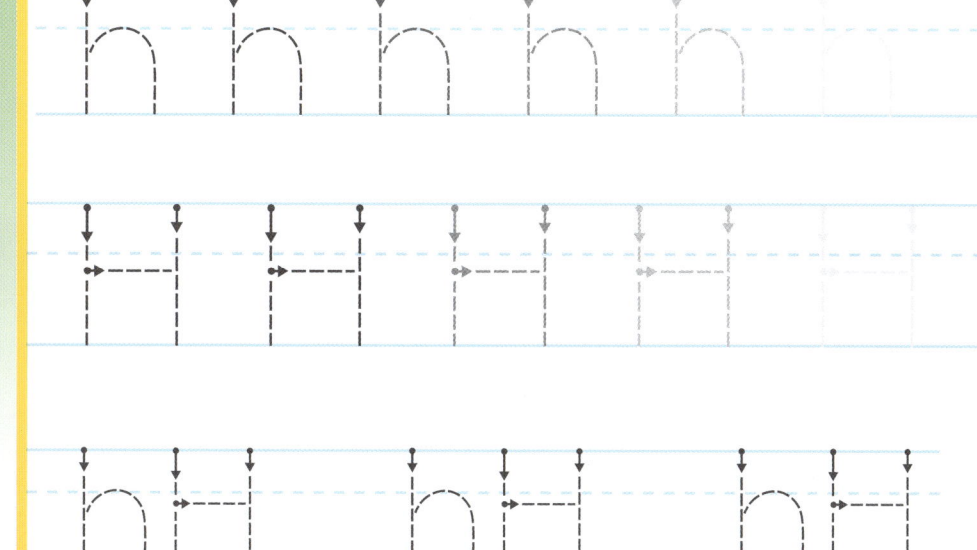

Let's try a sentence! Trace it, then copy it.

A hat on a horse.

11

Bring me to life!

Impy Ink

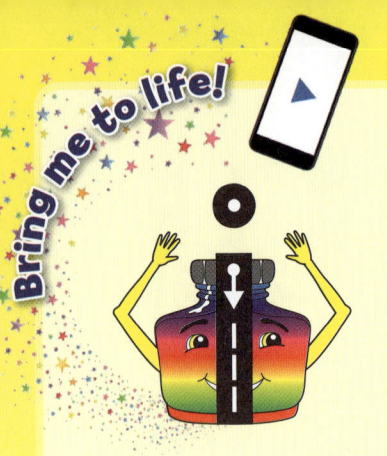

Inside the ink bottle
draw a line.
Add an inky dot.
That's fine!

Scan and sing the song, tracing the letter in the air, then write over the letter shapes below.

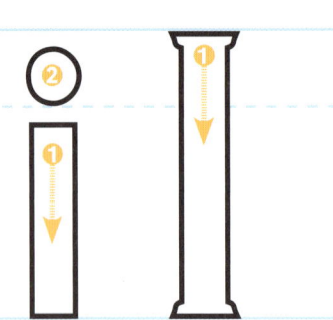

Impy Ink's pen
is a long, thin line.
Add two stands if you like.
That's fine!

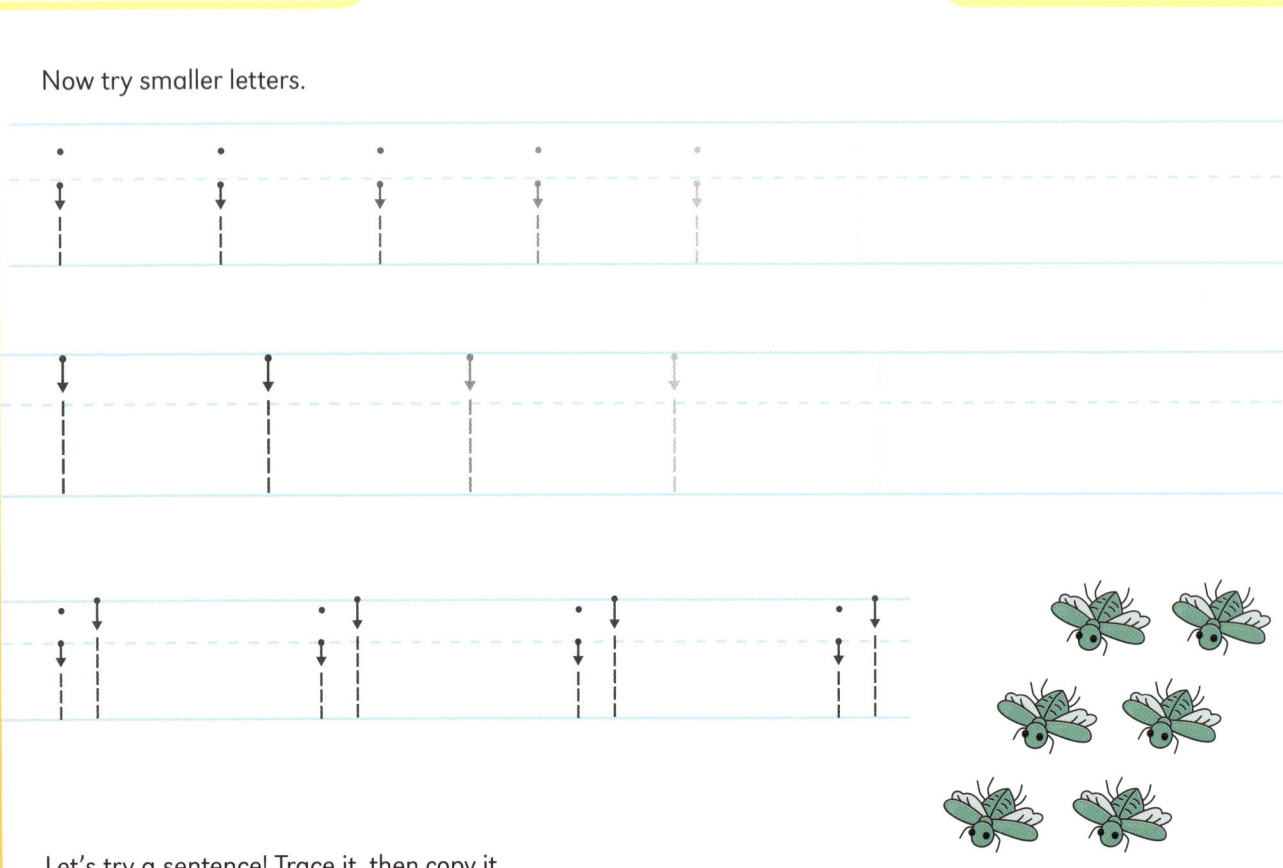

Now try smaller letters.

Let's try a sentence! Trace it, then copy it.

Six little insects.

Jumping Jim

Scan and sing the song, tracing the letter in the air, then write over the letter shapes below.

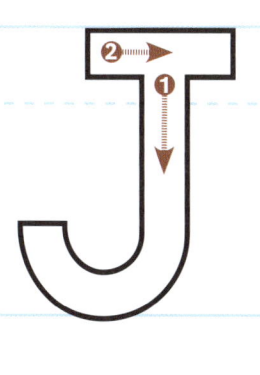

Just draw down Jim, bending his knees. Then add the one ball which everyone sees.

Jumping Jim can jump very high, so we can't see his head up in the sky. Go right down his body, bending his knees. For his arms add a line – which everyone sees!

Now try smaller letters.

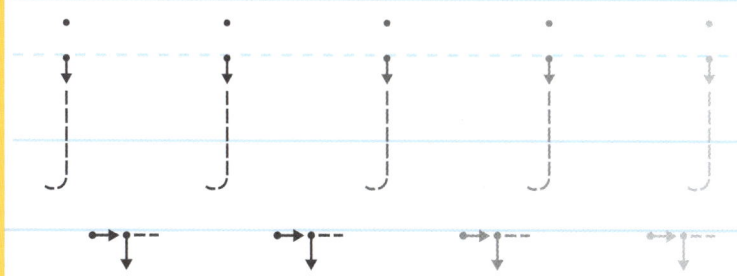

j j j j j

J J J J J

jJ jJ jJ jJ

Let's try a sentence! Trace it, then copy it.

A jug and jellies.

Bring me to life!

Kicking King

Scan and sing the song, tracing the letter in the air, then write over the letter shapes below.

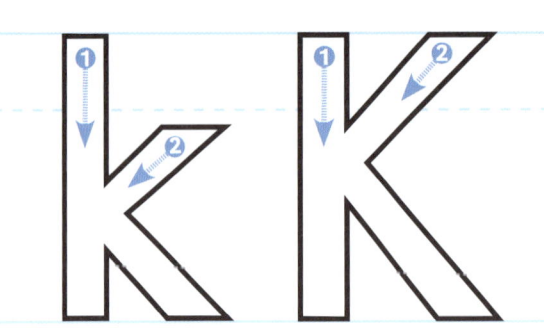

Kicking King's body is a straight stick. Add his arm, then his leg, so he can kick!

Kicking King's body is a straight stick. Make his arm and leg looooong for a really big KICK!

Now try smaller letters.

Let's try a sentence! Trace it, then copy it.

Kittens and keys.

14

Lucy Lamp Light

Scan and sing the song, tracing the letter in the air, then write over the letter shapes below.

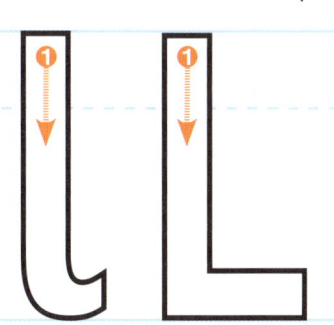

Lucy looks like one long line. Go straight from head to foot and she's ready to shine!

Lucy Lamp Light likes starting important words. That's when her legs grow quite long. Go straight down her body. Put her legs on the line. Do that – and you cannot go wrong!

Now try smaller letters.

l l l l l

L L L L L

lL lL lL

Let's try a sentence! Trace it, then copy it.

A lion and a log.

Bring me to life!

Munching Mike

Scan and sing the song, tracing the letter in the air, then write over the letter shapes below.

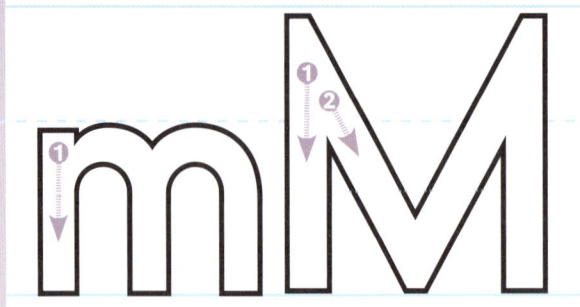

Make Munching Mike's back leg first, then his second leg, and third, so he can go munch-munching in a word.

Move from Mike's Mum's tail drawing down to her back wheel. At the top go down, up, and down again, so she can munch a big meal! Mmmm!

Now try smaller letters.

m m m m m

M M M M M

mM mM mM mM

Let's try a sentence! Trace it, then copy it.

A mug of milk.

Noisy Nick

'Now bang my nail,'
Noisy Nick said.
'Go up and over
around my head.'

Scan and sing the song, tracing the letter in the air, then write over the letter shapes below.

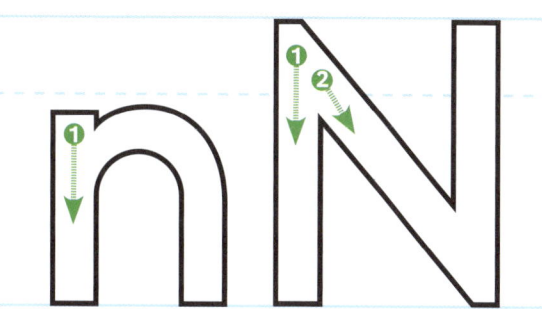

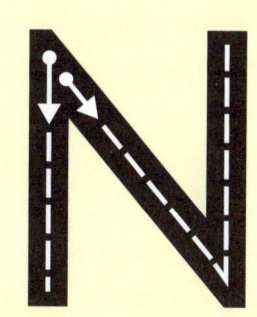

Noisy Nick's letter has three big nails: one..., and two... and three. Go down 1, go down 2, next up number 3 as quick as you can be!

Now try smaller letters.

Let's try a sentence! Trace it, then copy it.

Nine nice nuts.

Bring me to life!

Oscar Orange

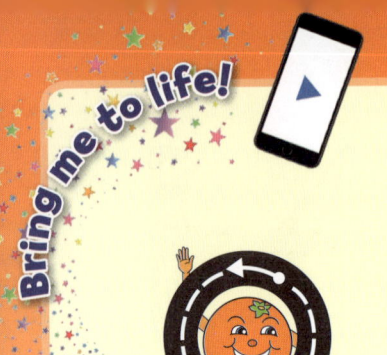

On Oscar Orange
start at the top.
Go all the way 'round him,
and... then stop.

Scan and sing the song, tracing the letter in the air, then write over the letter shapes below.

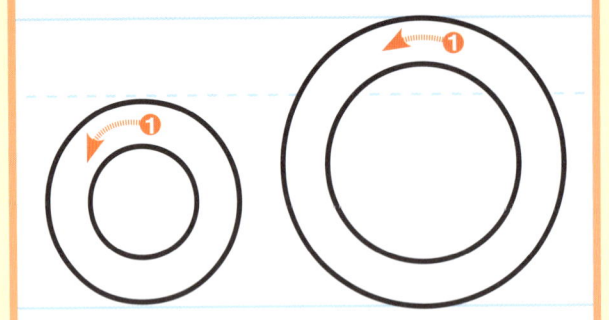

On Oscar Orange
start at the top.
Go all the way 'round him.
Make him BIG...
and then stop!

Now try smaller letters.

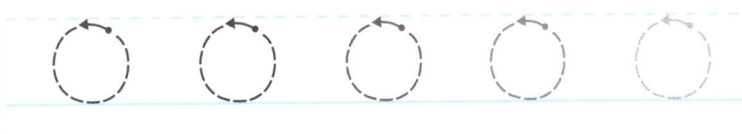

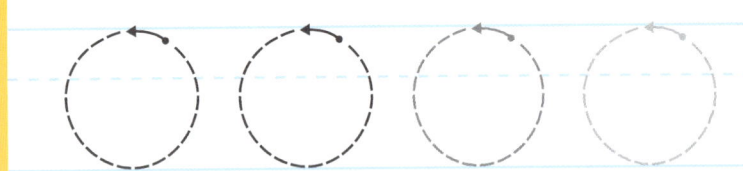

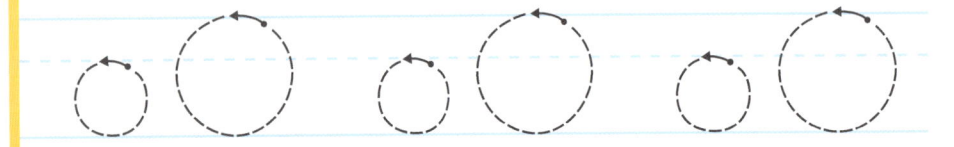

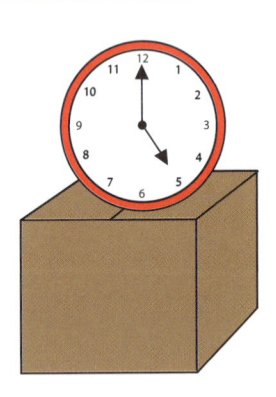

Let's try a sentence! Trace it, then copy it.

A clock on a box.

Peter Puppy

Scan and sing the song, tracing the letter in the air, then write over the letter shapes below.

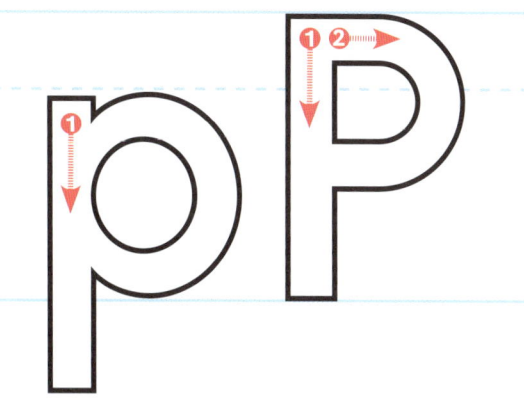

Pat Peter Puppy properly. First stroke down his ear, then up and 'round his face so he won't shed a tear.

Peter Puppy pops up for important words. From the back of his head go down to the ground. Then go right 'round his face so he'll whisper his sound.

Now try smaller letters.

p p p p p

P P P P P

pP   pP   pP

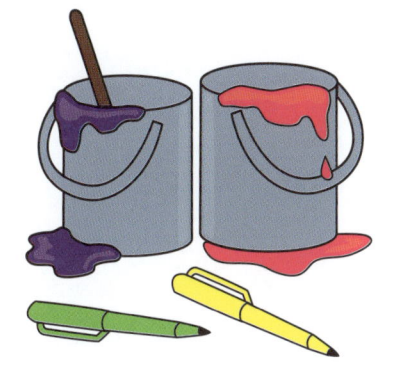

Let's try a sentence! Trace it, then copy it.

Pens and paint.

Bring me to life!

Quarrelsome Queen

Scan and sing the song, tracing the letter in the air, then write over the letter shapes below.

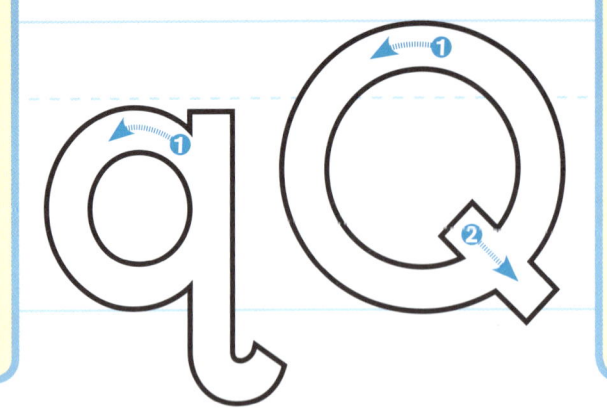

Quickly go 'round the Queen's cross face. Then comb her beautiful hair into place.

Quickly draw the Queen's Quiet Room. Make it cosy and round. Then add a place where she can sit whenever she needs to calm down.

Now try smaller letters.

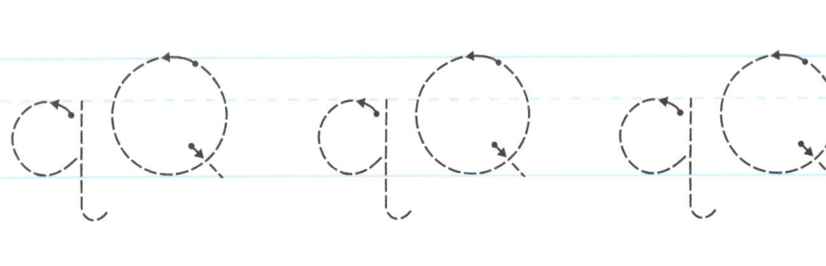

Let's try a sentence! Trace it, then copy it.

A queen's quilt.

Red Robot

Run down Red Robot's body. Go up to his arm and his hand. Then watch out for this robot roaming 'round Letterland.

Scan and sing the song, tracing the letter in the air, then write over the letter shapes below.

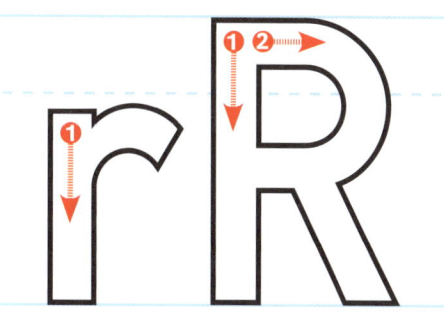

rR

Ready? Draw Red Robot's back and one leg that is straight. Add a curve, and another leg, so he's ready to roller skate!

Now try smaller letters.

r r r r

R R R R R

rR   rR   rR

Let's try a sentence! Trace it, then copy it.

Robots running.

Bring me to life!

Sammy Snake

Start at Sam's head where he can see. Stroke down to his tail, oh, so care-ful-ly!

Scan and sing the song, tracing the letter in the air, then write over the letter shapes below.

Start high on your page where Sammy Snake can see. Make his letter BIG, oh, so care-ful-ly!

Now try smaller letters.

Let's try a sentence! Trace it, then copy it.

Six spades on sand.

Talking Tess

Scan and sing the song, tracing the letter in the air, then write over the letter shapes below.

Tall as a tower make Talking Tess stand. Go from head to toe, and then from hand to hand.

Talking Tess can grow very tall. With her head in the clouds you can't see her at all. So draw a straight line from her neck to her feet, then another, left-to-right, for her arms, straight and neat.

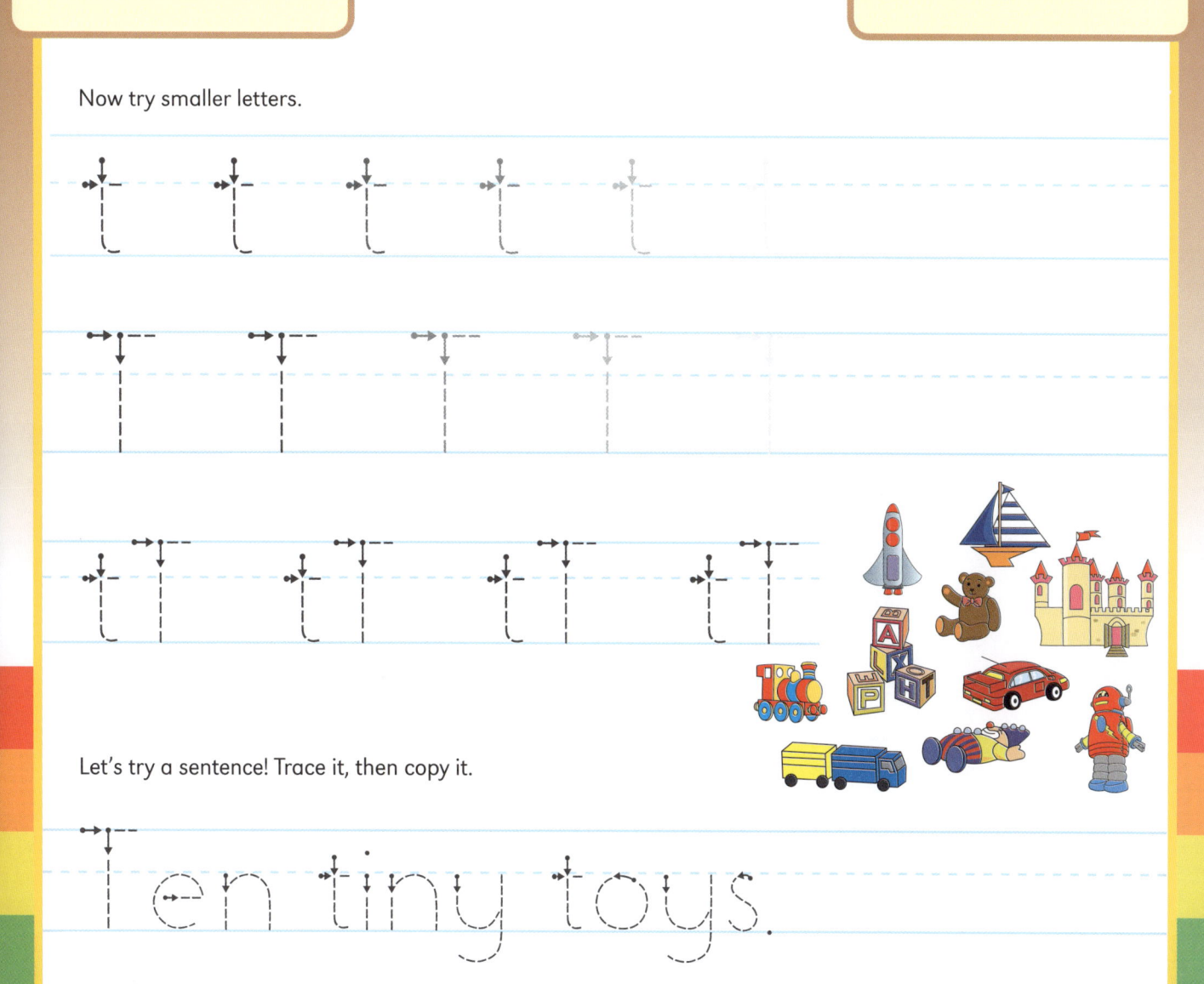

Now try smaller letters.

t t t t t

T T T T

tT tT tT tT

Let's try a sentence! Trace it, then copy it.

Ten tiny toys.

23

Uppy Umbrella

Bring me to life!

Under the umbrella draw a shape like a cup. Then draw a straight line so it won't tip up.

Scan and sing the song, tracing the letter in the air, then write over the letter shapes below.

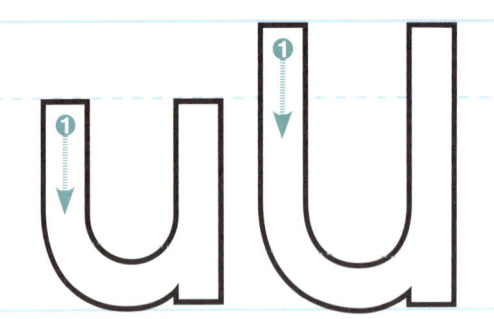

uU

Under Uppy Umbrella draw a BIG shape like a cup. Then draw a straight line all the way down so it won't tip up.

Now try smaller letters.

u u u u u

U U U U

uU uU uU

Let's try a sentence! Trace it, then copy it.

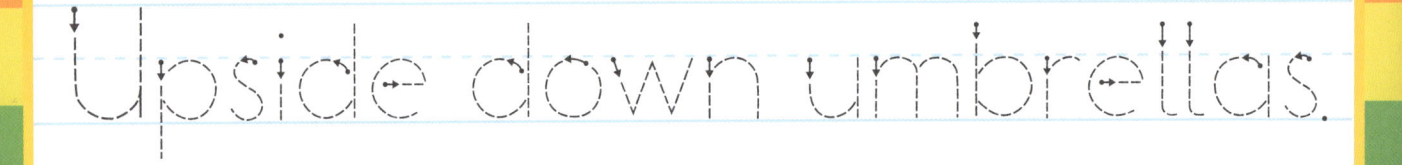

Upside down umbrellas.

Vicky Violet

**Very neatly,
start at the top.
Draw down your vase,
then up and stop.**

Scan and sing the song, tracing the letter in the air, then write over the letter shapes below.

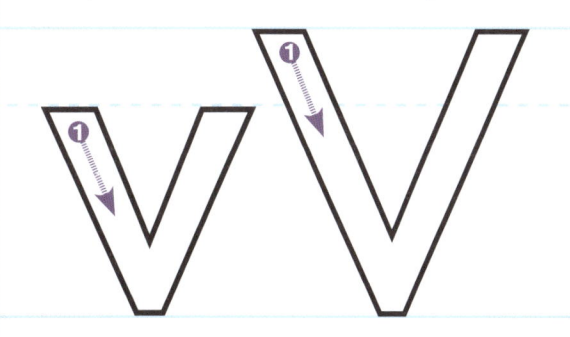

vV

**Vicky Violet has one
VERY BIG vase.
It's much bigger
than her little one.
Start at the top,
slant down to the line.
Draw back up to the top,
and it's done!**

Now try smaller letters.

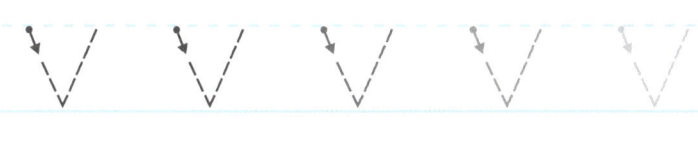

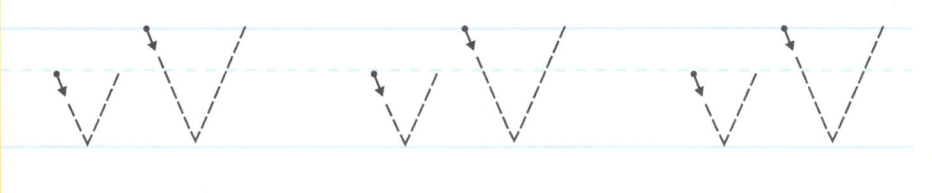

v v v v v

v v v v v

vv vv vv vv vv

Let's try a sentence! Trace it, then copy it.

A vegetable van.

25

Bring me to life!

Walter Walrus

When you draw the Walrus wells, with wild and wavy water, whizz down and up and then..., whizz down and up again.

Scan and sing the song, tracing the letter in the air, then write over the letter shapes below.

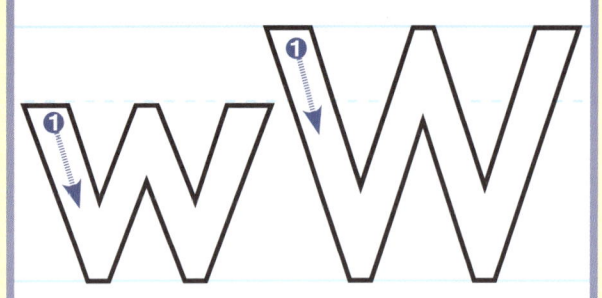

wW

When Walter Walrus wants BIG wells he takes a deep breath and he swells! So whizz down and up and then... whizz down and up again!

Now try smaller letters.

w w w w w

W W W W W

wW wW wW

Let's try a sentence! Trace it, then copy it.

A watch in a web.

Fix-it Max

Fix two sticks to look like this. That's how to draw a little kiss.

Scan and sing the song, tracing the letter in the air, then write over the letter shapes below.

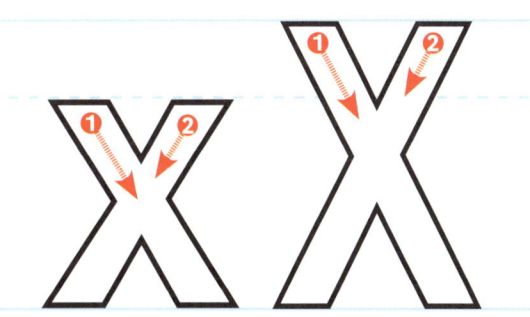

x X

Fix-it Max sends you a BIG kiss! Cross two big sticks to look like this!

Now try smaller letters.

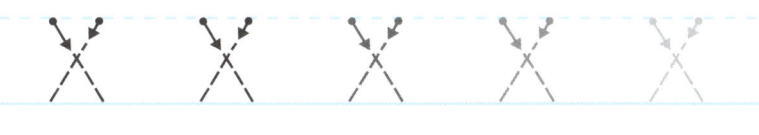

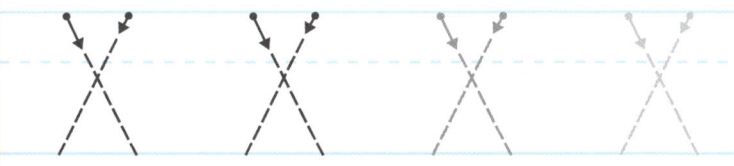

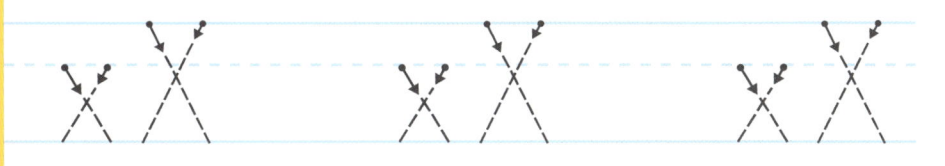

x x x x x

x x x x

xX xX xX

Let's try a sentence! Trace it, then copy it.

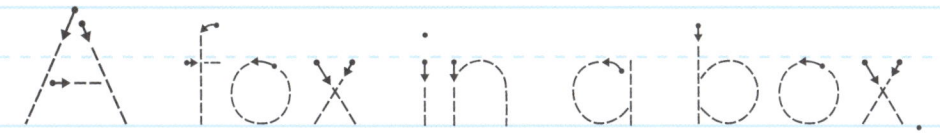

A fox in a box.

Bring me to life!

Yellow Yo-yo Man

Scan and sing the song, tracing the letter in the air, then write over the letter shapes below.

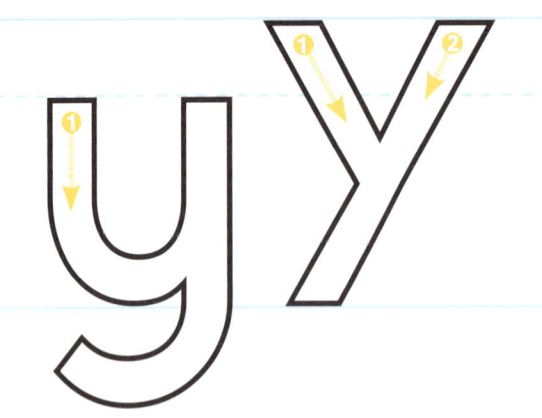

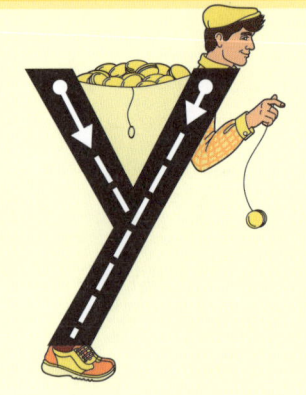

You first make the yo-yo sack on the Yo-yo Man's back, and then go down to his toes so he can sell his yo-yos.

Yes, start at the Yo-yo Man's sack. Go down that sack at the back. Then go down from his head to his toes, so he'll stand on the line to sell his yo-yos!

Now try smaller letters.

y y y y y

y y y y y

yy yy yy

Let's try a sentence! Trace it, then copy it.

"Yes, I like yellow!"

28

Zig Zag Zebra

Scan and sing the song, tracing the letter in the air, then write over the letter shapes below.

Zip along Zig Zag's nose.
Stroke her neck...,
stroke her back...
Zzzoom! Away she goes.

Zig Zag Zebra enjoys looking BIG, so give her a LONG nose, LONGER neck, and LONG back. Zzzoom! Away she goes.

Now try smaller letters.

z z z z z

Z Z Z Z Z

zZ zZ zZ zZ

Let's try a sentence! Trace it, then copy it.

A zebra at a zoo.

Aa-Zz Handwriting Practice

Let's trace all of the uppercase and lowercase letter shapes.

Reading Direction →

Aa Bb Cc Dd

Ee Ff Gg Hh

Ii Jj Kk Ll Mm

Nn Oo Pp Qq

Rr Ss Tt Uu Vv

Ww Xx Yy Zz

Numbers 1-10

Let's trace all of the numbers from 1 to 10.

1 one   6 six

2 two   7 seven

3 three   8 eight

4 four   9 nine

5 five   10 ten

Trace

1 2 3 4 5 6 7 8 9 10

Copy

a	b	c	d	e
Annie Apple	 Bouncy Ben	 Clever Cat	 Dippy Duck	 Eddy Elephant
f	g	h	i	j
 Firefighter Fred	 Golden Girl	 Harry Hat Man	 Impy Ink	 Jumping Jim
k	l	m	n	o	p
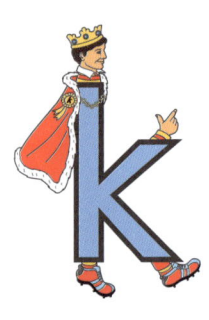 Kicking King	 Lucy Lamp Light	 Munching Mike	 Noisy Nick	 Oscar Orange	 Peter Puppy
q	r	s	t	u
 Quarrelsome Queen	 Red Robot	 Sammy Snake	 Talking Tess	 Uppy Umbrella
v	w	x	y	z
 Vicky Violet	 Walter Walrus	 Fix-it Max	 Yellow Yo-yo Man	 Zig Zag Zebra

www.letterland.com